Tali Pelman, KLN Productions and Arts at St. Ann's
present a Gate Theatre London production

WOYZECK
BY GEORG BÜCHNER
ADAPTED BY DANIEL KRAMER

Woyzeck was first performed at the Gate Theatre, London, on 8 November 2004.

ST. ANN'S WAREHOUSE
AT 38 WATER dumboBKLYN

WOYZECK
BY GEORG BÜCHNER
ADAPTED BY DANIEL KRAMER

in order of appearance:

Woyzeck **Edward Hogg**

Andres **Roger Evans**

Sergeant **Clive Brunt**

Drum Major **David Harewood**

Marie **Myriam Acharki**

Margaret **Rachel Lumberg**

Captain **Fred Pearson**

Doctor **Tony Guilfoyle**

Grandmother **Diana Payne-Myers**

Showman **Josh Cole**

Director **Daniel Kramer**

Set and Costume Designer **Neil Irish**

Lighting Designer **David Howe**

Sound Designer **Adrienne Quartly**

Choreographer **Ann Yee**

Assistant Director **Kendall O'Neill**

Production Manager **John Titcombe**

Stage Manager **Dan Ayling**

Costume Supervisor **Isabel Muñoz**

Aerial Movement **Gavin Marshall**

Aerial Training **Melissa Merran**

Military Consultant **Charles Mayer**

Supported by

BRITISH COUNCIL
United States

.and THE PETER JAY SHARP FOUNDATION

About The Play

Woyzeck is one of the most performed and influential plays in German theatre, widely recognized for its impact on writers as diverse as Kafka, Brecht and Beckett. The Prussian author, Georg Büchner, died in Zurich in 1837, aged 23, before the play was completed.

Büchner was born in 1813 in Hessen, Germany. While studying natural science and medicine in Strasbourg, he became politically involved and joined a student group that became the revolutionary 'Gesellschaft für Menschenrechte' (Society for Human Rights). In 1834, Büchner co-wrote an inflammatory political leaflet advocating the right of the peasants and the overthrow of the German princely states. The distribution of the leaflet led to a spurt of arrests, and Büchner, charged with treason, fled to France. While in exile, he wrote *Danton's Death* and *Leonce and Lena*. He died of typhoid fever just two years later.

Woyzeck was the first German literary work whose main characters were members of the working class. Büchner's play was inspired by the real life story of Johann Christian Woyzeck, who was beheaded in Leipzig in 1824 for the murder of his mistress. Prior to his execution, Woyzeck was interviewed by a doctor to determine whether he could be held responsible for his actions. In his writings, the doctor concluded that Woyzeck was 'of sound mind and that any abberations were due to his physical constitution and moral degeneration'.

Biographies

Myriam Acharki Marie

Myriam is Moroccan. She was born in Belgium where she trained and performed before coming to London to study with Phillippe Gaulier. **Theatre includes:** *Jane Eyre* (Shared Experience/Trafalgar Studios West End); *Woyzeck, Epitaph for the Whales, The Decameron* (Gate Theatre, London); *The Seven Year Itch* (London West End); *Macbeth False Memories* (ATC); *Princess Sharon* (Scarlet Theatre); *The Clayman* (El Innocente); *Murderer Hope of Woman* (Konkrete Theatre). **Television includes:** *Human Cargo* (CBC-Gemini Award Nominee); *Attachments, Holby City, Doctors, History Britain, Paradise Heights, Sex and Chocolate, Ella and the Mothers* (BBC); *North Square* (Channel Four). **Film includes:** *The Beach* (Figment Films/Fox).

Dan Ayling Stage Manager

Dan recently completed the MFA in Theatre Directing at Birkbeck College, London, having trained as a stage manager at Guildhall School of Music and Drama. **Directing:** *Can't Stand Up For Falling Down* (Arcola Theatre); *The Kiss* (Hampstead Theatre); *A Number* (Birkbeck). **Assistant Directing:** *Tales from Hollywood* (Perth Rep); *The Rubenstein Kiss* and *Nathan the Wise* (Hampstead Theatre); *Comfort Me With Apples* (Hampstead Theatre and UK national tour); *Fair* (Finborough Theatre and Trafalgar Studios); *Cricket Remixed* (Almeida Theatre); *Mary Stuart* (Drama Centre). **Assistant Producing:** *Beautiful Thing* (Sound Theatre). **Stage Management:** Seasons at Perth Rep, Pitlochry Festival Theatre, Citizens Theatre Glasgow, English National Opera and Almeida Opera.

Clive Brunt Sergeant

Clive trained at National Youth Theatre and East 15. **Theatre:** *Woyzeck* (Gate Theatre, London). **Television includes:** *Dunkirk Macbeth* (Shakespeare Retold), *The Echo, Nature Boy*. **Film includes:** *Pierrepoint* (The Last Hangman), *The Madness of King George*.

Josh Cole Showman

Theatre includes: *Kvetch, The Jew of Malta* (TDC, Milan); *Time to Jump* (ICA, London); *Behind Closed Doors* (Contact, Manchester); *Dumped* (Pleasance, Edinburgh). **Television includes:** *Robin Hood, Dirty War, Waste of Shame, Daniel Deronda, Strumpet* (BBC); *Dinotopia* (ABC/Hallmark); *Tough Love* (Granada); *Murder City, The Hunt, Ultimate Force* (ITV); *Sword of Honour* (Film Four); *Jack and the Beanstalk* (Jim Henson/Hallmark). **Film includes:** *The Beach, Crush, The Bunker, The Life and Death of Peter Sellars, Kinky Boots, The Lives of Saints*, plus the forthcoming *Right Hand Drive* and *Friends & Enemies*.

Roger Evans Andres

Roger trained at The Guildhall School of Music and Drama. **Theatre includes:** *Professor Bernhardi* (Oxford Stage Company); *Woyzeck* (Gate Theatre, London); *How Love is Spelt* (Bush Theatre); *Rose Bernd* (OSC); *The King Stag* (The Young Vic); *Art and Guff* (Soho Theatre); *Gas Station Angel, The Man Who Never...* (The Royal Court). **Television includes:** *Goldplated* (Granada); *Ghostboat* (Yorkshire); *Aberfan, Sea of Souls, Casualty, Doctors, Absolute Power, The Bench, Bradford in my Dreams* (BBC); *Murphy's Law* (Tiger Aspect); *Nuts and Bolts* (Carlton); *Mind to Kill* (Channel 5); *The Bill* (Thames); *Crime Traveller* (Carnival). **Film includes:** *Atonement* (Working Title), *Daddy's Girl* (Carnaby), *All or Nothing* (Thin Man Films), *Human Traffic* (Fruit Salad), *Suckerfish* (BBC).

Tony Guilfoyle Doctor

In New York: By LePage, *The Geometry Of Miracles* (Brooklyn Academy Of Music/World Tour); *KindertotenLieder* (The Lincoln Centre and Berlin) and *The Dragons Trilogy* (World Tour). **Other theatre includes:** *Shopping And Fucking* (Gielgud, The Queens and International Tour); *The Iceman Cometh* (Almieda

Theatre); *Shadow Mouth* (Sheffield Crucible); *The L.A. Plays* (Almeida Theatre); *Outskirts* (Royal Shakespeare Company); *Dealers Choice* (Clwyd); *San Diego* (Royal Lyceum/Edinburgh International Festival); *The Queen and I* (Out Of Joint); *Teorema* (Opera Della Roma, Queen Elizabeth Hall, Florence); *Imitation Of Life* (Bush Theatre); *If We Shadows* (Young Vic); *Translations* (Bristol Old Vic). **Film/television includes:** *Rome* (HBO), *Bleak House* (BBC), *The Virgin Queen* (BBC), *The Murder Of Stephen Lawrence* (Granada TV), *Father Ted* (Hat Trick), *Death Row. The Return. The Best Man* (Touchpaper).

David Harewood Drum Major

Trained at RADA. **Theatre includes:** *Othello, Henry IV, His Dark Materials* (National Theatre); *Antony and Cleopatra* (Public Theatre New York); *Julius Caesar* (Alley Theatre, Houston); *Romeo and Juliet* (Young Vic). **Television work:** *The Vice* (ITV), *BabyFather* (BBC), *Macbeth on the Estate* (BBC), *Ruby in the Smoke* (BBC), *Game On* (Channel 4), *Hearts and Minds* (Channel 4), *Silent Witness* (BBC). **Film credits include:** *Separate Lies, Merchant of Venice.* David is soon to be seen in the upcoming Warner Brothers film *Blood Diamond*, directed by Ed Zwick (*Last Samurai, Glory*).

Edward Hogg Woyzeck

Edward graduated from RADA in 2002. **Theatre includes:** *Rock 'n Roll* (Royal Court/Duke of York's Theatre); *The Storm, The Tempest, Measure for Measure* (Globe Theatre/St Ann's Warehouse, New York); *Woyzeck* (Gate Theatre, London – Ian Charleson Award Nomination); *The Pillowman* (National Theatre); *Loot* (Bristol Old Vic); *The Silver Sword* (Nottingham Playhouse); *The Firemaker's Daughter* (Sheffield Crucible); *King Lear* (Royal Shakespeare Company). **Film includes:** *Brothers of The Head, Song of Songs, Alfie, Nicholas Nickleby.* **Television includes:** *The Bermuda Triangle: Beneath the Waves* (BBC); *Celeb* (Tiger Aspect) and *Heartbeat* (Granada). **Radio includes:** *Boxing Clever, Sgt. Musgrave's Dance* and *Metropolis* (all BBC Radio 4).

David Howe Lighting Designer

Selected design credits include: **Broadway:** *Primo* (Music Box Theatre), recreation of the original National Theatre design. **West End lighting design credits include:** *Seven Brides for Seven Brothers* (Haymarket); *Pageant* (Vaudeville Theatre); *Forbidden Broadway* (Albery Theatre); *The Last Five Years* (Menier Chocolate Factory); *Rags* (Bridewell Theatre) and *La serva padrona* (Royal Opera House). **Current UK national tours include:** Disney's *Beauty and the Beast* and *Me and My Girl.* **Previously with Daniel Kramer:** *Orestes 2.0* (Guildhall). **International design work:** *English Speaking Theatre* (Frankfurt); *Stars of the Musicals* (Malaysia); *Sunset Boulevard* (Cork Opera House); *Who Shot the Sheriff & Dracula* (Tivoli, Copenhagen); *Jesus Christ Superstar* (Tour of Sweden) and many other productions around Europe. **As Associate Lighting Designer:** *Lord of the Rings* (Toronto and London); *The Woman In White* (West End & Broadway); *Hamlet* (Old Vic); *Humble Boy* (West End & UK Tour); *Nine* (West End and Buenos Aries); *Electra* (UK Tour & West End); the National Theatre's *Carousel* (West End and Japanese Tours).

Neil Irish
Set and Costume Designer

Neil trained in Birmingham and later at The Slade in London and the National Film and TV school. **Previous productions seen in Brooklyn:** Handel's *Rodelinda and Amadigi* (Brooklyn Academy of Music). **Recent productions in UK include:** *Hard Times, Vertigo, Get Carter, The Third Man, Moby Dick, Sweeny Todd, Merlin the Winter King, Kafka's Letters* (UK Tours). **Recent operatic projects include:** *Carmen* (New Zealand); *Hyacinthus* (Dublin, London, Buxton, Cannes and Rome); *Vera Of Las Vegas* (OTC Dublin); *Pagliacci* (English Touring Opera/Pegasuss Opera (UK Tour); *The Nightingale's to Blame* (Opera North). Neil has also worked for BBC TV Birmingham Set and Costume Departments. Forthcoming productions include Arthur Miller's *The Price* (UK Tour).

Daniel Kramer Adapter/Director

Daniel is currently a Creative Associate at the Royal Shakespeare Company and an Associate Director at the Gate Theatre, Notting Hill. **Theatre credits include:** *Bent* starring Alan Cumming (Trafalgar Studio 1, West End); *Hair* (Gate Theatre, London); *Woyzeck* (Gate Theatre, London); *Through the Leaves* starring Ann Mitchell and Simon Callow (Duchess Theatre, West End and Southwark Playhouse); *Romeo and Juliet* (St George's Theatre, London; the Al Bustan Festival, Lebanon); *The Crucifixion*, a York Mystery Play (Blue Heron Theatre, NYC); *Blood on the Cat's Neck*, *The Quiet Game*, *The Sorcerer's Apprentice* (Hangar Theatre Lab, Ithaca, NY – 1999 Drama League Fellowship). **Devised theatre credits include:** *Sweet Charity Too* (Royal Shakespeare Company); *Punch and Judy* (London Arts Council Playwriting Grant); *Funhouse* (NYC Fringe Festival).

Rachel Lumberg Margaret

Training: Guildhall School Of Music & Drama. **Theatre includes:** *Chatsky* (Almeida Theatre); *Peace In Our Time* (British No.1 Tour); *Katherine Howard* (Chichester Festival Theatre); Victoria Wood's *Talent* (Colchester Theatre); Alan Ayckbourn's *Between Mouthfuls* (Colchester Theatre); *See How They Run* (Salisbury Playhouse); *Woyzeck* (Gate Theatre, London); *Il Turco In Italia*, *Le Nozze Di Figaro* (The Royal Opera House). **Television includes:** *Undercover Heart*, *The Moonstone*, *Tears Before Bedtime*, *Sunburn*, *Holby City*, *Hetty Wainthropp*, *Accused*, *A Lump in my Throat*, *Casualty* (all for BBC); *A Touch Of Frost* (ITV); *A Dance To The Music Of Time* (Channel 4). **Film:** *Emma* (Matchmaker Films), *South Kensington* (Medusa Films), *Get me to the Crematorium* (Leda Serene Films). **Radio:** *Henry IV part 1* (BBC Radio 4).

Gavin Marshall Aerial Movement

Aerial choreography includes: *Henry VI pts 1–3, The Tempest, 12th Night, Pericles* (Royal Shakespeare Company); *Spellbound* (Club Archaos); *Tumbling After* (Camden Council). **Theatre includes (acting):** *Henry VI pts 1-3, Richard III* (Royal Shakespeare Company); *Trainspotting* (Ambassadors Theatre); *Coriolanus* (Steven Berkoff); *Gormenghast* (David Glass Ensemble); *Cyrano de Bergerac* (Communicado); *Marabou Stork Nightmares* (Leicester Haymarket); *7 Sonnets* (Lyric Hammersmith); *Crimes of Passion* (Nottingham Playhouse); *Sleeping Beauty* (Edinburgh Lyceum); *Beauty and the Beast* (Dundee Rep). **Direction includes:** *Tales of An Extravagant Stranger* (Royal Shakespeare Company); *Spellbound* (Club Archaos); *Berkoff's Women* (Leicester Haymarket); *No Fear, Believe* (Linda Marlowe Productions); *Conspiracy Cabaret* (David Benson).

Isabel Muñoz
Costume Supervisor

Isabel trained in Set and Costume design and graduated from University of Central England in 2001. **Design work includes:** *The Return and Collision* (Birmingham Stage Company at The Old Red Lion Theatre); *Deadly Nightcap* (Vienna's English Theatre); *Desdemona* (Hill Street Theatre); *Simpatico* (White Bear). **Costume work includes:** *The Persian Revolution* (Lyric Hammersmith Studio); *Majnoun* (Riverside Studios); *The Dice House* (Arts Theatre); *Under the Curse* (Gate Theatre, London); *Exclude Me* (The Chelsea Theatre). **As Design Assistant:** *Nicholas Nickleby* (RedShift Theatre); *Lady Chatterley's Lover* (Hull Truck Theatre). **Film includes:** *Tincture of Vervain, We're Ready for You Now* (Pathetique films).

Kendall O'Neill
Assistant Director

New York directing credits include: *The Smiths* (West End Theatre); *About the Rabbits* (Producers Club); *Faulty But Not Broken* (Belly). **Assistant Directing credits include:** *Gasping* (Haymarket Theatre Basingstoke); *The Persians* (Perry Street Theatre); *Everything Will Be Different* (Soho Rep); *Cabaret & Main* (Williamstown Theatre Festival); *The Dream Express* (The Zipper Theatre); *Like I Say* (The Flea Theatre). **Administrative/ Producer credits:** *Gizmo Love* (ATC

London/Edinburgh Festival); *The Factory Girls* (Arcola Theatre) and for Manhattan Theatre Club.

Diana Payne-Myers
Grandmother

Training: Marie Rambert, Mercury Theatre, Notting Hill Gate, London. Danced in Nijinsky Gala, Earl's Court, 1949. **1950s:** trained, performed in pantomimes, variety, West End musicals, television and cabaret. **1960s–1980s:** taught choreography and established workshops and seminars. **1980s–2006:** worked as a freelance dancer and actress. Returned in the 1980s as a freelance dancer with choreographers such as Phillipe Découfflé (Bicentaire Champs-Elysées Paris, 1989); Matthew Hawkins; Lloyd Newson (DV8 Physical Theatre Company); Quinny Sacks (David Pountney's Fairy Queen for ENO). **Theatre includes:** *Baby Doll* (National Theatre); Caryl Churchill's *The Skriker* (National Theatre) and Stephen Daldry's *An Inspector Calls* (Garrick Theatre). **Film includes:** *Boxes* (dir. Jane Birkin). At present Diana is working with Matthew Hawkins and The Imminent Dancer's Group. 200 MBE Services to Dance.

Fred Pearson Captain

Theatre includes: *Much Ado About Nothing, The Caucasian Chalk Circle, Our Friends in The North, The Prince of Homberg* (Royal Shakespeare Company); *A Fair Quarrel, King Lear, Pravda, The Government Inspector, Futurists* (National Theatre); *Hysteria* (Duke of York's Theatre). **Television includes:** *Wives and Daughters, Middlemarch, Dalziel and Pasco, The Bill, Midsomer Murders, The Nuclear Race* (to be released).

Adrienne Quartly
Sound Designer

Theatre includes: *93.2FM* (Royal Court Theatre, London); *Hideaway* (Complicite); *Playing For Time, A Touch Of The Sun* (Salisbury Playhouse, UK); *Mercy Fine* (Clean Break Theatre); *Tejas Verdes* (Gate Theatre, London); *Attempts On Her Life, Hysteria* (Battersea Arts Centre, London);

Lady Luck (Edinburgh Festival); *Jarman Garden, Inflated Ideas* (Riverside Studios, London); *Last Waltz Season* (Oxford Stage Company). **Cellist:** *Artist Rifles* (Piano Magic); *National Alien Office* (Riverside Studios). Music compiler for Gut Records UK.

John Titcombe
Production Manager

John was Production Manager at Hampstead Theatre for eight years. Since then freelance projects include: *Pool (no water)* (Plymouth / Frantic Assembly); *An Hour and a Half Late* (Bath / UK Tour); *Look Back In Anger* (Peter Hall Season, Bath); *My Fair Lady* (Larnaca International Festival, Cyprus); *An Enemy of the People* (UK Tour / Tara Arts); *Present Laughter* (Bath / UK Tour); *Mammals* (Bush / UK Tour); *Aladdin* (Greenwich Theatre); *Longitude* (Greenwich Theatre); *Playing with Fire* (National Theatre); *What the Butler Saw* (Criterion Theatre); *Aristocrats* (National Theatre); *Losing Louis* (Trafalgar Studios West End); *Bat Boy the Musical* (Shaftesbury Theatre).

Ann Yee
Choreographer

Training: Bachelors of Fine Arts in Dance from The Boston Conservatory, Master's of Fine Arts in Dance from The Ohio State University. **Recent work as movement director or choreographer includes:** *Bent* (Trafalgar Studio 1, West End); *Big Love* (Gate Theatre, London); *Food* (Traverse Theatre, Edinburgh, Fringe First Award 2006); *The Odyssey* (Lyric Hammersmith, Bristol Old Vic); *Lysistrata* (Arcola Theatre); *The Magic Carpet* (Lyric Hammersmith); *Sweet Charity Too: The Workshop Showing* (Royal Shakespeare Company); *Hair* (Gate Theatre, London); *Sex, Chips, Rock and Roll* (Manchester Royal Exchange); *Orestes 2.0* (Guildhall School of Music and Drama); *Woyzeck* (Gate Theatre, London).

Producers

Tali Pelman

Ms. Pelman, formerly Producer and Associate Artistic Director of London's Gate Theatre, is now an independent theatre producer.

As Producer credits include: *The Emperor Jones* (directed by Thea Sharrock, designed by Richard Hudson, starring Paterson Joseph); the first present-day adaptation of iconic musical *Hair* (adapted by the authors, directed by Daniel Kramer); Fermín Cabal's *Tejas Verdes* (directed by Thea Sharrock, designed by Dick Bird); the multi-award winning *Woyzeck*; Lara Foot Newton's *Tshepang* from the Baxter Theater in Cape Town; *The Arab-Israeli Cookbook* (co-produced by Caird Company, starring Sheila Hancock) and The Civilians' *Gone Missing* (Galapagos Arts Space New York/London Gate Theatre transfer).

Raised in South Africa, Israel and London, Ms. Pelman is a graduate of Columbia University and the London School of Economics.

Kay Ellen Consolver

Founder of KLN Productions, a London based theatrical production company, specializing in new writing and innovative interpretations of classics.

Productions: *Tabloid Caligula* (Arcola Theatre, London; Brits off Broadway Festival, New York City); *Belfast Blues* (Soho Theatre).

Underwriting: For the Gate Theatre: *Woyzeck* and *Hair*, directed by Daniel Kramer, and *Emperor Jones* directed by Thea Sharrock; *Catch* (Royal Court Theatre); Edinburgh Festival award winning productions *Missing Persons* (2005), including London transfer to Trafalgar Studios, and *Take Me Away* (2004) London transfer to Bush Theatre; *Three Women and a Piano Tuner* (Hampstead Theatre); *Through the Leaves* (Southwark Playhouse/Duchess Theatre) directed by Daniel Kramer.

Patron: Gate Theatre, Donmar Warehouse, Royal Court Theatre (Production Syndicate), Royal National Theatre and Tricycle Theatre.

Board Memberships: Tricycle Theatre (Development Board); The Playground (London based theatre devising network); Executive Board, LAMDA, the UK's oldest drama school; Studio Theatre, Washington, DC.

St. Ann's Warehouse

Producer

Founded in 1980, Arts at St. Ann's (ASA) is an award-winning presenting/producing organization that relocated to DUMBO on the Brooklyn Waterfront in 2001. Its flexible, 14,000 sq foot venue, St. Ann's Warehouse, provides an artistic home for the American avant-garde, young international companies, and emerging/mid career artists in need of a creative producer and production team. A pioneer in theatricalizing music presentation and developing distinguished crossover projects, ASA has made its reputation creating hybrid interdisciplinary work based in music and theater. Notable productions include Lou Reed and John Cale's *Songs for 'Drella*, *Mabou Mines' Peter and Wendy* and *Dollhouse*, and *Theater of the New Ear* by filmmakers Charlie Kaufman, The Coen Brothers and composer Carter Burwell. In 2004, ASA was awarded the Ross Wetzsteon Memorial Award for the development of new work, describing St. Ann's Warehouse as "an inspiring laboratory" where a "super-informed audience charges the atmosphere with hip vitality."

Arts at St. Ann's Board of Directors:

Anthony D. Schlesinger, *Chairman*

Ronald E. Feiner

Susan Feldman, *President*

Frances Kazan

Thomas T. Newell

Steven B. Rissman, *Assistant Treasurer*

Joseph S. Steinberg

David Wagner, *Vice President*

David Walentas

Susan Feldman Artistic Director

Sallie D. Sanders General Manager

Marilynn Donini Director of External Affairs

Owen Hughes Production Manager

Alex Berg Business Manager

Bill Updegraff Marketing Manager

Bill Kennedy Technical Director

Karl C. Sturk Box Office Manager

Aaron Rosenblum Production Coordinator

George Bixby Marketing/Development Associate

Mitchell D. Sickon Assistant Box Office Manager

Laura Sadai Management Associate

Mark Berger Intern

The Gate Theatre

Original Producer

The Gate Theatre in Notting Hill occupies a unique place in London and British theatre and has done for over 27 years, as the only company dedicated to international work. The Gate is a small, ambitious theatre known for its inventive use of space and the exceptional artists it attracts.

An environment in which artists can create first-class and original theatre, The Gate provides the structure and support necessary for emerging talent to develop. Encouraging artistic risks which might not be possible in larger organisations, the Gate is a springboard for opportunity allowing emerging artists to excel and make their mark. With an audience capacity of between fifty and seventy people, the space has challenged and inspired directors and designers, making it famous for being one of the most flexible and transformable spaces in London.

The Gate has been home to many artists including Jude Law, Alex Kingston, Rachel Weisz, Kathy Burke, Sir Peter Hall, Sarah Kane, Katie Mitchell, Nancy Meckler, Mick Gordon, and Ian Rickson. It is "one of the major generators of theatrical talent in this country". (*Stephen Daldry, Former Artistic Director of the Gate, Director of* Billy Elliot).

The Gate relies on artistic dedication and the generous support of individuals. Never deterred by financial limitations, the Gate continues to break boundaries and present the very best in world theatre.

For more information on the Gate's work and how to support it, please visit **www.gatetheatre.co.uk**.

Artistic Director **Thea Sharrock**

Producer **Evanna Meehan**

General Manager **Cath Longman**

Technical Manager **Nick Abbott**

Fundraising & Events Co-ordinator **Henriette Krarup**

Literary Manager **Claire Lovett**

Finance Assistant **Steve Woods**

Education Officer **Lynne Gagliano**

General Assistant **Lauretta Barrow**

Gateink Coordinator **Lloyd Wood**

Box Office **Paul Long & Stewart Melton**

Associate Directors **Daniel Kramer & Anna Mackmin**

The Gate Theatre Board of Trustees are: **Kevin Cahill** (Chair), **Jonathan Hull** (Secretary), **Pim Baxter, Mark Bayley, Diane Borger,** Rupert Christiansen, Susan Hitch, **Rima Horton** and **Colin Simon**

The Gate is supported by Arts Council England

Gate Theatre

11 Pembridge Road, Notting Hill, London W11 3HQ, United Kingdom

Box Office +44 (0)20 7229 0706

Administration +44 (0)20 7229 5387

Fax +44 (0)20 7221 6055   www.gatetheatre.co.uk

Georg Büchner

WOYZECK

Adapted by
Daniel Kramer

OBERON BOOKS
LONDON

First published in 2006 by Oberon Books Ltd
521 Caledonian Road, London N7 9RH
Tel: 020 7607 3637 / Fax: 020 7607 3629
e-mail: info@oberonbooks.com
www.oberonbooks.com

A catalogue record for this book is available from the British
Library.

ISBN: 1 84002 705 3 / 978-1-84002-705-1

Printed in Great Britain by Antony Rowe Ltd, Chippenham

A note on this adaptation

Georg Büchner died before *Woyzeck* was completed – or perhaps his final manuscript was lost during the tragedy of his young death. Either way, no one truly knows in what exact order Büchner finally intended his scenes to be played. This freedom was my starting point and, I think, should be every artist's starting point with *Woyzeck*: what story do *you* see in these scenes? The following version uses the order I arranged for my production at the Gate in London in 2004, but I have intentionally cut all references to my realization of the scenes and the production itself, as I think that the profundity of this play lies in its ruins. And it's the readers', the director's, the production team's, the actors' job to use *their* understanding and vision to express the story. If my adaptation can be of use to any artist – wonderful. But please do rearrange, cut, paste, add… Make it *your* story. Make it speak to you. To your audience.

D.K. 2006

Characters

CAPTAIN ALEXANDER
head of the garrisoned regiment

DOCTOR FRANZ CHRISTIAN AUGUST CLARUS / A HORSE
the regimental doctor

THE DRUM MAJOR

SERGEANT SCHMIDT

WOYZECK
a fusilier and orderly to the Captain

ANDRES MÜLLER / A MONKEY
a fusilier and Woyzeck's friend

MARIE
Woyzeck's common-law wife
and the mother of Christian, his son

MARGARET
Marie's neighbour

GRANDMOTHER / A CAT
Woyzeck's grandmother

A TRAVELLING SHOWMAN

CHRISTIAN
Marie's and Woyzeck's baby

This adaptation of *Woyzeck* was first performed on 8 November 2004 at the Gate Theatre, London, with the following company:

CAPTAIN, Fred Pearson

DOCTOR, Tony Guilfoyle

DRUM MAJOR, Tim Chipping

SERGEANT, Clive Brunt

WOYZECK, Edward Hogg

ANDRES, Roger Evans

MARIE, Myriam Acharki

MARGARET, Rachel Lumberg

GRANDMOTHER, Diana Payne-Myers

SHOWMAN, Josh Cole

Directed by Daniel Kramer
Designed by Neil Irish
Choregraphy by Ann Yee
Lighting by Charles Balfour
Sound by Adrienne Quartly

SCENE ONE

THE WOODS

WOYZECK: Andres – you know this place is cursed? Do you see that pale strip of grass there where the toadstools are? A head rolls down there every evening. Once upon a time, there was a man picked it up, thought it was a hedgehog: three days 'n' three nights later, he was lying in his coffin. (*Quietly; a revelation.*) Andres, that was the Freemasons, it was, the Freemasons.

ANDRES: (*Whistling a tune.*)

WOYZECK: Quiet. Can you hear that, Andres? Can you hear that? Something's movin': behind me, beneath me. (*Stamps on the ground.*) Hollow, do y' hear that? Everything's hollow down there. The Freemasons.

ANDRES: You're scaring me, Woyzeck.

WOYZECK: (*Returns to work.*) Strange silence. Makes y' wanna hold your breath. (*Pause.*) Andres!

ANDRES: What?

WOYZECK: Say something. (*WOYZECK stares into the dawning sky.*) Andres, look how bright. Everything's glowing above the town. 'And the angel took the censer and cast it unto the earth: and there were voices, thundering, and lightning, followed by hail and fire mingled with blood…'

It's coming towards us, Andres. Quick!

He drags ANDRES aside.

Don't look behind you!

ANDRES: (*After a pause.*) Woyzeck, can you still hear it?

WOYZECK: Silence, nothing but silence. As if the world was dead.

An alarm bell rings in the distance.

ANDRES: Do you hear that? Reveille. (*Pronounced 'rah-valley'.*) We gotta go to roll-call.

INTERLUDE
ROLL-CALL

SERGEANT: RIGHT. MARKERS.
MARKERS. STEADY.
GET ON! PARADE!
RIGHT DRESS.
EYES. FRONT.
STAND AT. EASE.
Come to attention and answer your names. Fusiliers Müller.

ANDRES: (*Coming to attention.*) SERGEANT. (*Standing at ease.*)

SERGEANT: Woyzeck.

WOYZECK: (*Coming to attention.*) SERGEANT. (*Standing at ease.*)

The DRUM MAJOR enters.

SERGEANT: COMPANY SHUN.
Good morning, Sir. C Company is present and awaiting your inspection.

DRUM MAJOR: No time this morning, Sergeant. TO YOUR DUTIES. (*Beat.*) DISS – (*Beat.*) MISSED.

WOYZECK and ANDRES exit with the sticks.

Piss off Schmidt.

The SERGEANT exits. The DRUM MAJOR turns to reveal himself.

SCENE TWO
THE WINDOW OF MARIE'S HOME & THE ADJACENT STREET

Enter MARIE and her baby, CHRISTIAN, at a window.

MARIE: (*Singing.*) Un peu triste
       Un peu têtue
       Mets ton pardessus
       Solitude danse enronds…

Eh, bon matin, mon grand! Comment que tu va?

Military drums in the distance.

Ah – do you hear that? Here he comes!

The DRUM MAJOR begins to march towards MARIE. MARGARET plows onstage and right into the DRUM MAJOR's path. MARGARET scurries down to MARIE's window.

MARGARET: Oh, what a man. Like a tree.

MARIE: Like a lion.

The DRUM MAJOR marches towards the ladies and salutes MARIE before exiting.

MARGARET: Well, well, well Marie – what friendly eyes we have today. It's not every one of us gets such a warm and neighbourly welcome from you now, is it?

MARIE: How does the song go? (*Singing.*) Soldiers, they are handsome lads.

Both laugh.

MARGARET: Marie – look at your eyes – they're still shinin'.

MARIE: And? Take yours out and polish them. Then maybe they'll shine a bit. And you'll have something *worth* selling. On the corner.

MARGARET: Oh that's rich, coming from you. Mrs I'm-a-virgin-with-a-child-and-no-wedding-ring. I am a respectable woman, I am, everyone knows that, but you…your eyes could see through seven pairs of leather trousers.

MARIE: Eh, oh! Ça va. Catin.

MARIE yanks the curtain closed; MARGARET plods off. The baby cries.

Shhhh, shhhhh. Let them say what they want. It doesn't matter. Tu seras toujours mon amour et mon ange.

> (*Singing.*) Tire le tapis de sous moi
> Et tu me deliveras
> Pousse-moi
> Je m'en fous
> Je ne pese rien du tout
> Pirouettes sur le parquet
> Pirouettes à jamais

WOYZECK knocks at the window.

Who's there? Is that you, Franz? Come in!

WOYZECK: (*Kisses her and smiles.*) Can't. (*WOYZECK holds up all of the sticks.*)

MARIE: The Captain?

WOYZECK: Yeah.

MARIE: Are you all right?

WOYZECK: It happened again, Marie. A lot. Isn't it written, 'And lo, there arose a smoke out of the land like the smoke out of a furnace'?

MARIE: Franz…

WOYZECK: It followed me to the edge of town. Something I…can't understand, can't grasp, something that…takes away all sense. When's it going to end, Marie?

MARIE: Shhhh, shh.

WOYZECK: I gotta go… Travellin' show's in town tonight. And I saved up some money again. Do y' wanna go?

MARIE: Yes!

WOYZECK runs to work; MARIE, watching him from a distance:

Franz. What is happening to him? His mind is on fire. He didn't even glance at his own boy. Too haunted by these…thoughts. And why are you so quiet, mon grand, uh? Are you scared? So dark, it's like going blind. No light today but a street lamp. I can't stand it. I'm rotting.

SCENE THREE
THE CAPTAIN'S

The CAPTAIN enters.

CAPTAIN: Slowly, Woyzeck, slowly; one thing after another. You're making me ill. What am I supposed to do with the ten minutes *you* save by rushing? Think about it, Woyzeck: you have a good…thirty years ahead of you – thirty years! That's three hundred and sixty months. And then there's days, hours, minutes, seconds.

What will you do with all that time? Such an immense amount of time. Pace yourself, Woyzeck.

WOYZECK: Yes Sir.

CAPTAIN: It makes me rather frightened for the world when I think of eternity. Too much business, Woyzeck, too much bus-y-ness. Eternity is…eternity, yes? And yet it's not. It's a moment. A single moment. It terrifies me, Woyzeck, to think the entire world turns round on its axis in one day. What a waste of *time*. And where's it going to end, Woyzeck, how's it going to end? I can barely look at a wheel anymore without getting depressed.

WOYZECK: Yes Sir.

CAPTAIN: You always look so…hunted, Woyzeck. A good man doesn't look like that…a good man…a good man, with a good, clear conscience… Well say something, Woyzeck… What's the weather like today?

WOYZECK: Bad, Sir, bad: windy.

CAPTAIN: Yes, I've felt it all morning: terribly chilling out there. Gives me goose-pimples just thinking about it. Like thinking of rats. (*Shivers and contorts; then, craftily.*) I reckon it's a northerly-southerly wind, Woyzeck. What do you think?

WOYZECK: Yes Sir.

CAPTAIN: Ha, ha, ha! Northerly-southerly! Ha, ha, ha! Oh, you are stupid, quite abominably stupid! (*Touched.*) Ahhh – you're such a good man, Woyzeck, such a good man. Though, (*With dignity.*) you don't have any morals, Woyzeck. Morals…morals are…well – when one is moral, yes? It's an important word, Woyzeck. You have a child without the church's blessing – as our reverend garrison padre says: 'without the church's blessing'. You'll excuse me, it's not my expression.

WOYZECK: I don't think God'll refuse to let the poor little fella into heaven just because no one said 'amen' when he was made. Sir. Jesus said, 'Suffer the little children to come unto me'.

CAPTAIN: What did you just say? Not what Jesus said, what *you* said.

WOYZECK: Well…if you're poor like me…you know what I mean, Sir? Money, it's about money. If you don't have money – just try to get someone of my class into the world in a…'moral' way. And just because we don't have any money doesn't mean we aren't made of flesh and blood, too… No. We're unblessed in this world and the next. And I expect if any of us *did* get into Heaven, they'd put us to work on the thunder.

CAPTAIN: But that doesn't mean you can't have virtue, Woyzeck. And you're not a virtuous man. Flesh and blood. When I lie by my window after a nice calming rain and see a pair of little white stockings go skipping down the street, dammit, Woyzeck, I lust, too. I'm made of flesh and blood, too. But, virtue, Woyzeck, my virtue. I say to myself: 'You are a virtuous man, (*Touched.*) a moral man, a *good* man.'

WOYZECK: Yes, Sir: virtue. I don't think I've quite got that one. I think…people of my class don't have virtue, we just…do what nature tells us to. But if I was a gentleman and had a watch and a frock-coat and I had your accent – I'd be virtuous. I'd be really *really* virtuous. It must be a wonderful thing to be virtuous, Sir. But I'm just…poor.

CAPTAIN: (*Genuinely moved by WOYZECK's sentiment.*) Hm. You're such a good man, Woyzeck. Such a good, good man. Though you think too much. And it wears you out. That's why you always look so shaken. Now, this conversation has exhausted me. Get on your way, but *please don't run.* Walk slowly, nice and slowly down the street. I'll see you this afternoon at tea.

WOYZECK: (*Saluting the CAPTAIN.*) Good morning, Sir.

CAPTAIN: Thank you.

> *The CAPTAIN gives WOYZECK a coin. WOYZECK walks away – slowly.*

SCENE FOUR
THE DOCTOR'S OFFICE

The DOCTOR enters and sees WOYZECK urinating against a wall in the street.

WOYZECK: (*Saluting the DOCTOR.*) Good morning, Sir.

DOCTOR: What do I see before me, Woyzeck? A man of his word?

WOYZECK: Excuse me, Sir?

DOCTOR: I saw it, Woyzeck, I saw it with my own eyes: you! Pissing in the street. Pissing against a wall. Like a dog. A dog! Is this what I pay you and feed you for? Hm? No, Woyzeck, no. This is bad, Woyzeck, very bad. People like you are making the world a bad place to live in.

WOYZECK: But, Sir…when nature calls.

DOCTOR: When nature calls, when nature calls. Nature! That is superstition, Woyzeck, pure, abominable superstition. Was it not I who proved that the *musculus constrictor vesicae* is subject to the will? Nature. Man is free, Woyzeck. In man, individuality is embodied in its most perfect expression: freedom. Not able to control your own bladder – ha! (*Begins his physical examination of WOYZECK.*) Have you eaten your peas today, Woyzeck? Remember: nothing but peas…*Cruciferae*! Or is it *Leguminosae*? Hm. I'm going to revolutionize science, Woyzeck, I'm going to blow the whole thing sky high! Now, according to yesterday's chart: uric acid, 0.10; ammonium hydrochlorate, hyperoxide – Any chance you need to piss again, Woyzeck? Go on. Go on. TRY.

WOYZECK goes behind the screen and tries to urinate.

WOYZECK: I can't, Sir.

DOCTOR: But you can piss in the street! Against a wall, like a DOG! I saw it with my eyes, my very own eyes: I had just finished with my *Valnersia* and *Myrodie,* when I opened the window and stuck my nose out to let the sun-rays fall upon my face in order to observe the stimuli behind the sneezing process: *ratio sternutamentis* – When all of a sudden – &\$@%!!!! Or should I say psssssssss…sss sss sssss! WE HAD A URINARY AGREEMENT, WOYZECK. *IN WRITING!!!* No. No. I will not be angry. Anger is unhealthy. Anger is unscientific. I am calm and in control. Completely in control. My pulse is its usual sixty, and I am speaking to you in the most cold-blooded manner possible. Why anyone would allow themselves to be upset by another human being is beyond – and beneath – me. If it had been the death of one of my precious lizards, my *Lacerta…* Nonetheless, Woyzeck, you shouldn't have pissed in the street. Against a wall. Like a dog.

WOYZECK: Well, Sir, sometimes some people are just…
that way, have that kind of character, that kinda…make-
up. Like me. Nature is…something different. It's
something…how do you say? Well, for example –

DOCTOR: Woyzeck, you're philosophizing again.

WOYZECK: Sir, have you ever seen nature's *other side*?

DOCTOR: The other side of nature, Woyzeck?.

WOYZECK: The other side of nature, that's it, the *other
side* of nature: when the world becomes so dark you've
got to grope your way around, and you feel like the
whole world's… (*Does poetic gesture with hands that
expresses 'disintegrating'.*) …like a spider's web in your
hands… Like when something exists but doesn't exist…
(*WOYZECK begins to stride up and down the room.*) When
everything is pitch black and yet there's this red glow in
the West…when /

DOCTOR: Good God, Woyzeck, you're crawling about like
a spider.

WOYZECK: The toadstools, Sir – that's it! It's all in the
toadstools – have you ever noticed how they grow in
rings on the ground: long lines, silent circles…figures –
Patterns! Patterns! It's there in the patterns! If someone
could just…read those… (*A secret:*) When the sun stands
still at midday and blazes like it's going to devour the
world in fire, a terrible voice speaks to me.

DOCTOR: Woyzeck, you have the most beautiful *aberratio
mentalis partialis* of the second level – fixed ideas but a
generally rational condition. Very beautifully distinct.
The second level. Very uniquely distinct, Woyzeck!
Oh, my theory, my precious theory. I'm going to be
immortalized, Woyzeck! Immortalized! I'm giving you

a bonus, Woyzeck! I'm giving you a bonus! Have you completed all of your work this morning?

WOYZECK: Yes Sir.

DOCTOR: Eating your peas?

WOYZECK: Yes Sir. I save the money for Marie and Christian.

DOCTOR: Fulfilling of your duties for the Captain?

WOYZECK: Yes Sir.

DOCTOR: You're an interesting case, Subject Woyzeck. Here's your bonus. (*DOCTOR hands WOYZECK a coin.*) Keep up the good work. Ah, let me just take your pulse before you go. I must have your pulse every morning and every night. Yes! Yes!! YES!!!

Alarm bell rings.

WOYZECK: Good morning, Sir.

INTERLUDE
WORK

MARIE, GRANDMOTHER, MARGARET and ANDRES clean the CAPTAIN's tea towels. WOYZECK serves the CAPTAIN tea. The SERGEANT inspects the workers. The DRUM MAJOR works out.

WOYZECK: Good evening, Sir.

CAPTAIN: Good evening.

SCENE FIVE

THE TRAVELLING SHOW JUST OUTSIDE TOWN

WOYZECK takes MARIE to the Travelling Show. The SHOWMAN sets his tent up.

MONKEY: (*Lots of overexcited, loud, chimpanzee noise.*)

SHOWMAN: Shut up! (*To a worm.*) 'Thou know'st 'tis common: all that lives must die, Passing through Nature to Eternity.' (*Eats the worm.*)

WOYZECK: What a way to start an evening.

MARIE: The poor man is a wise man.

WOYZECK: Look at those eyes – such pain turned to such joy.

MARIE: Strange world, beautiful world.

SHOWMAN: Ladies and Gentlemen, step right up, the smallest show on earth is about to begin! We have beasts as God created them; we have beasts as man created them. Regardez: (*Gesturing to his crippled body.*) the animal as God created it: nothing. Nothing at all. But see you now l'Art – Art – the beast as man created it: (*MONKEY enters dressed as a soldier and marches around.*) he walks upright, wears a jacket, pantalons and cap; he even carries a little sword! Mais oui! The monkey is a soldier – zhe lowest form of life on earth, no? Take a bow, soldier.

MONKEY bows.

Et voilà, now he is a Captain. Come on then, luv, give us a kiss. Un bisou!

MONKEY kisses SHOWMAN. MONKEY shows his joy by imitating the alarm bell sound.

Et voilà – il joue le reveille – rah-valley – time for work! And don't you be late (*SHOWMAN goes to hit MONKEY.*) Mesdames et Messieurs – zhe soldier!

All applaud; MONKEY exits.

Et maintenant, Mesdames et Messieurs, step right in to see zhe astronomical, mathematical, super-grand cheval – (*Aside to the likes of WOYZECK.*) a big horsie who counts, eh!?! – plus ze world's plus petites clairvoyantes: les oiseaux! Tweet tweet tweet. Favourèd by dhe crownèd heads of Europe. Let them tell you your fortune: when will you marry, how many children will you have, when will they die, when will you die, how will you die… (*He seems to be speaking directly to MARIE; snaps out of it.*) Mesdames et Messieurs, zhe greatest show on earth iz about to begin! C'est le commencement du commencement. Venez – entrez!

WOYZECK: Do y' want to go in?

MARIE: I don't care.

WOYZECK holds a coin out to MARIE.

Yes!

WOYZECK and MARIE go to pay the SHOWMAN. The DRUM MAJOR and SERGEANT stroll onstage.

DRUM MAJOR: Stop. (*Beat.*) Look. At. That.

SERGEANT: Jesus Christ. She could rear an army.

DRUM MAJOR: And breed a whole race of Drum Majors.

SERGEANT: Look at that chin in the air. You'd think that black mane'd drag her down.

DRUM MAJOR: And those eyes. Like staring into Hell. Come on.

The DRUM MAJOR walks straight past the SHOWMAN, leaving the SERGEANT to pay. The SHOWMAN opens the tent. MARIE is immersed in a sea of light and fantastical objects a poor unmarried woman might love.

MARIE: Oh – light!

WOYZECK: (*Seeing the DRUM MAJOR across the space.*) Black cats with fiery eyes. Dangerous night.

SHOWMAN: (*Leading a wild HORSE to the pedestal.*) Viens mon brave, show zem your talents! Show zem your intelligence bestial. Put dem all to shame – all of la société humaine to shame! Mesdames et Messieurs, dis animale you see before you – tail, hooves and all – is a member of the highest learned societés du monde, a professeur à l'université where he teaches his students Mounting et Riding, eh!?! Mais oui, ça c'est la raison, n'est-ce pas? Bestiality. I mean, Beastology. But think you now...à l'inverse. Zhe ozer way! Backwards! This is no stupid animale: this is un individuale, a person, a human being, an animalised human being, oui – But always, a human being. Et une bête.

The HORSE defecates.

Mais voici, put dem all to shame – all of la société humaine to shame. You see? The animale *obeys* the laws of nature. Unspoilt nature. Ask your doctor, much more harmful to hold it in! And thus it is said: Man, be naturelle. From dust, sand and filth were you created. And so why would you want to be more? How can we be? C'est un-raisonnable. You want reason? I'll show you reason. This horse here before you can do arithmetic but he can't even count on his fingers. How, you ask me. Because even though he can't express himself, can't explain himself, he is still a human being – simply different. Transformé. Regardez: mon brave, s'il vous plaît, dites les Messieurs-Dames quelle heure est-il. Mesdames et Messieurs, is there any one amongst you who has a watch? A watch?

The DRUM MAJOR and SERGEANT get rid of WOYZECK. The DRUM MAJOR buys MARIE a pair of beautiful earrings. MARIE heads home with CHRISTIAN.

SCENE SIX
MARIE'S HOME

MARIE enters near the window with her BABY.

MARIE: The Sergeant gives him an order, he has to go. Again.

She settles on her windowsill, takes the earrings out and puts them on, and then admires herself with a shard of broken mirror.

Look how they shine! What kind are they…ce qu'il m'a dit?… Sleep, mon grand. Close your eyes. Tighter! Tighter, or the ogre'll get you!

> (*Singing.*) Tire le tapis de sous moi
> Et tu me deliveras
> Pousse-moi
> Je m'en fous
> Je ne pese rien du tout
> Pirouettes sur le parquet
> Pirouettes à jamais

(*Looks in mirror again.*) They must be diamonds. How they will shine when I'm dancing? Ha! All I am supposed to have is a corner of earth. And a piece of mirror. But my lips are as red as those upper-class ladies' with their gold-framed mirrors and their handsome white gentlemen, kissing their delicate, gloved hands. Moi – a *poor* girl.

The BABY cries.

(*Harshly.*) Quiet! (*Then softly.*) Close your eyes! Vite! Or the ogre'll see you, and you'll go blind.

WOYZECK: What's that?

MARIE: Nothing.

WOYZECK: Something's shining under your fingers.

MARIE: An earring. I found it.

WOYZECK: I never found anything like that. Two at once.

MARIE: So you think I'm lying?

WOYZECK: No, no, it's… I'm / I'm… Look at him sleeping. Move his little arm; he's pressing up against it. Bright beads a' sweat all over his forehead. Nothing but work under the sun. We even sweat in our sleep. Here's the rest of my money, Marie: my wage and a bit extra from the Captain.

MARIE: Thank you, Franz.

WOYZECK: I… I gotta get back to the barracks. I'll see you tomorrow. Good night.

MARIE: (*Alone, after a pause.*) Oh – I am evil. I deserve to die. (*Beat.*) It doesn't matter. The whole world's going to Hell: every man and woman in it.

MARIE exits. WOYZECK left alone eating peas as the lights fade to blackout.

SCENE SEVEN
THE DOCTOR'S OFFICE & MARIE'S HOME

The DOCTOR enters the space followed by WOYZECK holding a CAT. The scene is actually two separate scenes played in the same space.

DOCTOR: Ladies and Gentlemen, I stand upon this platform this morning like David when he spied upon Bathsheba. Though all I can see is the garden of the girls' school with their knickers drying on the line. Anyway, Ladies and Gentlemen, we come this morning to the important question of the relationship between the Subject / …

The DRUM MAJOR enters.

DRUM MAJOR: Marie.

DOCTOR: … / and the Object.

MARIE: (*Entering the space.*) Quick march.

DOCTOR: Observe Specimen A: a common house-cat.

CAT: Meow!!!

The DRUM MAJOR marches in a circle around them all.

DOCTOR: In whom the Divine organically manifests and thereby affirms itself.

MARIE: Bull's chest. Stallion's thighs. There's no one else on earth like him.

DOCTOR: And let us now examine its relationship to its environment, to the earth and to the universe.

MARIE: And he chooses *me*!

DOCTOR: Ladies and Gentlemen, when I throw this *felis* out of the window,

The CAT hisses at the DOCTOR.

how, according to the laws of its *centrum gravitationis,* will it instinctually behave?

DRUM MAJOR: You should see me on Sundays /

DOCTOR: (*As the CAT swipes at WOYZECK.*) Woyzeck!

DRUM MAJOR: With my thick feather plume and my clean white gloves.

DOCTOR: (*Shouting as the CAT bites at WOYZECK.*) Woyzeck!

DRUM MAJOR: 'Jesus Christ,' the Prince says when he sees me…

WOYZECK: Sir, it's biting me.

DRUM MAJOR: 'That's a Man.'

DOCTOR: Well, you're holding it like a girl.

The DOCTOR crosses to take the CAT from WOYZECK. MARIE crosses to DRUM MAJOR.

MARIE: (*Mocking him.*) Oh really. (*Nose to nose with him.*) A man.

DRUM MAJOR: And you, a woman.

WOYZECK: (*Aside to DOCTOR.*) Sir, I've got the shakes.

DOCTOR: Oh. (*Rather delighted.*) OH!!! This is wonderful, Woyzeck, just wonderful! Gentlemen, this beast has no scientific instinct.

The DOCTOR takes the CAT from WOYZECK and throws it to the ground. The CAT screeches and exits.

CAT: Meow!

The DRUM MAJOR seizes MARIE in his arms – it is passionate and somewhat violent; but not abusive or the violence of rape – a sexual domination that MARIE clearly craves, lacks and desires. This instantly changes into a tender, deep, passionate kiss.

DRUM MAJOR: My God, I want t' create a whole battalion of drum majors with you.

The DOCTOR places WOYZECK on the pedestal.

DOCTOR: Gentlemen, observe Specimen B: for the past three months this *homo sapiens* has eaten nothing but peas. Let us now examine the effects: irregular pulse, cloudy eyes…

As the kissing ecstasy heightens, WOYZECK's faintness intensifies.

WOYZECK: Sir, everything's going dark. (*He goes to sit down.*)

DOCTOR: Hold it!

MARIE: Get out!

MARIE shoves the DRUM MAJOR away. He raises his hands in the air like a gentleman and backs away, giving her space – never losing eye contact. She backs away to the opposite wall.

DOCTOR: Just a little longer and it will all be over. Now, oh, wait – Woyzeck, you have to wiggle your ears for them.

DRUM MAJOR: You're a wild animal.

DOCTOR: Ladies and Gentlemen, observe Specimen B isolating and moving two traditionally involuntary muscles as, hitherto, only quadrupeds have been known to do. Woyzeck, wiggle!

MARIE: (*Unable to control herself; full of desire and need.*) Touch me.

DOCTOR: Now!

The DRUM MAJOR, MARIE and the DOCTOR spiral round each other with WOYZECK in the centre of it all. The DRUM MAJOR lifts MARIE in his arms and spins her to the ground. They kiss.

WOYZECK: (*Over the above, to himself.*) Please stop, please.

DOCTOR: You stupid beast, do you want me to move your ears for you?

DRUM MAJOR: Look at those eyes. Is that the Devil I see?

DOCTOR: Note, Ladies and Gentlemen, his progressive transformation into an *asellus,* the common consequence of an all-female upbringing and a lack of education. How many hairs has your mother tenderly ripped out as a souvenir of her love today, Woyzeck, hm? Getting awfully thin up there. Or is it just the peas, Woyzeck, the peas?

MARIE: (*To herself as the DRUM MAJOR undoes her corset.*) It doesn't matter.

DOCTOR: Ladies and Gentlemen...

MARIE: It's all the same.

DOCTOR: The peas!

Orgasm. The DRUM MAJOR rushes off. MARIE slowly re-dresses and exits. WOYZECK hurries off to MARIE's. WOYZECK goes to exit without saluting the DOCTOR.

Woyzeck!

WOYZECK: (*Saluting.*) Good afternoon, Sir.

SCENE EIGHT
THE STREET

WOYZECK runs off. The DOCTOR begins to go when suddenly the CAPTAIN explodes into the space after him:

CAPTAIN: August – don't run so quickly! You're making me ill waving your cane all about like that. Besides, the only thing you could be chasing that quickly is your death. A good man, with a good clear conscience, does not run so quickly. A good man – (*He clutches onto the DOCTOR.*) August, permit *me* to save a human life today.

DOCTOR: I'm in a rush, Alexander, I'm in a rush. (*He struggles to break free.*)

CAPTAIN: I'm depressed, August, I'm depressed. My imagination's gone wild. I cry all of the time. When I see my coat hanging on the wall, I / (*On the verge of losing it.*)

DOCTOR: All right. All right. Hm, yes: sweaty, feverish, scant of breath, eyes jaundiced, tongue woolly. Yes. Yes. The apoplectic type, Alexander. You're a prime candidate for an *Apoplexia cerebri* – an apoplectic seizure of the brain. Of course, it *is* possible that you might only be affected down *one* side of the body – *hemi-paresis*. Or in the best-case scenario, you might only have *local* cerebral paralysis – mental paralysis. In which case you'd spend the rest of your life as a sort of human vegetable. Hm, yes. Those are pretty much your prospects for the next four weeks. *Though*, you could become a truly unique case and, God willing, have only *part* of your tongue become paralyzed. Now, in that case, we could do experiments that would immortalize us both!

CAPTAIN: August, please don't frighten me. There are people – I've read about people who have died of terror, pure and utter terror. I can already see everyone at my funeral, standing over my grave. But listen, can you hear what they're saying: (*A huge smile and tears come over his face.*) 'He was a *good* man. A *good* man.' May the Devil pound the last nail in your coffin.

DOCTOR: (*Behaves like a child imitating a human vegetable.*) What's this, Alexander? This is you post your mental paralysis.

CAPTAIN: (*Ripping the DOCTOR's military badge off.*) And what is this, August? That is you and your career after I have you drummed out of the regiment!

CAPTAIN unleashes his huge laughter; the DOCTOR goes white.

Ha, ha, ha! Oh! No offence, August! I'm a *good* man, but I can give as good as I get! Ha, ha, ha! When I want! Ha! If I want! Ha, Ha!

WOYZECK comes rushing by.

Woyzeck! Why are you hurrying past us like that? Come here for a second. You run through the world like an open razor – you're going to cut someone someday. Why, you run as if you had a regiment of eunuchs to shave and would be hanged if a stray hair were found. A propos hair… How do I say this? Woyzeck /

DOCTOR: As the great Roman philosopher Pliny said, 'Hair should be discouraged amongst soldiers'.

CAPTAIN: Hm, yes, Pliny, thank you. Returning to the subject of hair. Woyzeck, you haven't, by any chance, found someone else's hair in your *soup* lately, have you?

Do you...know what I mean? A hair from...another man? From a...certain private, or sergeant, or...a, ah...drum major? Woyzeck? Hello?

WOYZECK boils.

But no, you've got a good girl, Woyzeck, haven't you. Not like all the others, huh!

WOYZECK: Yes, Sir. What are you trying to say, Sir?

CAPTAIN: Look at the poor fella's face. All right, forget about the soup, Woyzeck, but...if you hurry round the corner, you might just find a certain drum major on a certain pair of lips. A familiar pair of lips, Woyzeck. To you, I mean.

WOYZECK begins to alter.

Listen, I've... I've been in love before, too, Woyzeck. It's / Dear me, Woyzeck, you're turning white!

WOYZECK: (*Emotion we have not seen in him before.*) I'm a poor man, Sir. She's all I have. So if you're making fun of me, Sir, please stop.

CAPTAIN: Making fun of you? Me? Do you think I would find this funny?

DOCTOR: Your pulse, Woyzeck, your pulse! Low, hard, violent, irregular.

WOYZECK: Sir, the earth's as hot as Hell but I'm ice ice cold... So. Bet you Hell is cold. (*Beginning to break, on his knees, mouthing the words to the Heavens.*) Impossible. Please please. (*He breaks with a pang of epic emotion.*) IMPOSSIBLE!

CAPTAIN: Fusilier Woyzeck, do you / do you want a bullet through your skull? How dare you look at me like that.

CONTAIN YOUR EMOTIONS. I am trying to help you because I think you are a good man, Woyzeck, a *good* man.

DOCTOR: Facial muscles rigid, tense, occasionally twitching. Spine erect, nervous.

WOYZECK: Gotta go, Sir. Everything is possible. (*Pang – he begins to eat peas non-stop.*) NO! Everything is possible. Oh, we have such beautiful weather here, Sir. I mean, just look at that thick grey sky: makes you kinda want t' put a nail in it and hang yourself, doesn't it? And all because of that little word, 'yes'. And again, 'YES'. And 'no'! 'Yes' and 'no', Sir. But is the 'no' to blame for the 'yes' or the 'yes' for the 'no'? I need to think about that.

Exits.

DOCTOR: (*Runs after WOYZECK.*) Phenomenal, Woyzeck! I'm giving you a bonus!!!

CAPTAIN: Oh, I'd better go after them. Not that I want to. A good man is cautious and values his life. A good man is not courageous. Dogs are courageous; dogs go to war for courage. It's grotesque. Grotesque! I only went to war to affirm my love of life.

The CAPTAIN follows after WOYZECK and the DOCTOR.

SCENE NINE
MARIE'S HOME

WOYZECK: Ahhh!!!! I can't see anything, I can't see anything! You should be able to see it. You should be able to grab it with your hands! You should be able to /

MARIE: Franz, what is wrong with you; what / What are you talking about?

WOYZECK: What a nice house. What a nice place to live. What a nice place to have company.

MARIE: What?

WOYZECK: A lotta people pass by this window, don't they, Marie? Huh? And you can talk with them, and…to whoever you choose, right? And it's…got nothing to do with me, does it? No / Did he stand there? There? There there there? And you here, here. Like this? Huh? Well…? I wish I'd been him.

MARIE: Him? Wha/ Who / What are you talking about, Franz? I can't stop people from walking down the street. Or looking in my window or…force them to stop talking to me.

WOYZECK: Or force them to leave their *lips* at home? (*To himself.*) It would be such a shame; lips so beautiful perfect. My favourite part. A feasting ground for wasps.

MARIE: Franz, you're scaring me, what is going on?

WOYZECK: Sin. A sin. So black and fat, its stench could kill all the little angels of Heaven. That red red mouth a yours, Marie; no blisters on it yet? Oh – how is it possible you're as beautiful as sin? I wonder: is mortal sin so beautiful?

MARIE: You're ill, Franz, you're ill.

WOYZECK: And you're the Devil. Did he stand here? (*Aggressively; rubbing against her.*) Like this? Like this?

MARIE: Well, being that so many people walk down the street, and stop at my window, and talk with me – I obviously invite them into my house; because, as you said, it is such a nice place to live, such a nice place to have company. So *anyone* could have stood there.

WOYZECK: (*Stilled.*) I see him.

MARIE: You can see a lot of things if you have two eyes, are not blind, and the sun is shining.

WOYZECK: SLUT! (*Goes to attack her.*)

MARIE: (*Opening herself to him in a most terrifying manner.*) GO ON! TOUCH ME! *TOUCH ME.* No man hits me since the day I turn ten years old and could look my father in the eye. And I rather have a knife in my heart than your hands on me… Get out. GET OUT.

WOYZECK exits into the street. MARIE leans against her window, crying.

WOYZECK: (*In the street, turning back to MARIE's window and throwing his money at her.*) WHORE!!! No, no, it'd show in her face. Ugh, everyone's an abyss, and it makes me ill lookin' inside. Rightfully so. She stood there like the picture of innocence. Innocence, you got a stain on your dress. You're marked. Am I sure though, am I sure? Who's ever sure?

SCENE TEN
THE BARRACKS

ANDRES getting dressed.

WOYZECK: Andres!

ANDRES: Yes?

WOYZECK: …Nice weather this evening.

ANDRES: Yeah. Everyone's going out tonight – you wanna come?

WOYZECK: (*Restless.*) Dancin', Andres, are they goin' dancin'?

ANDRES: The Lodge.

WOYZECK: Dancin' and dancin'.

ANDRES: Yeah…

WOYZECK: I'm not doing well, Andres.

ANDRES: Oh really.

WOYZECK: I gotta go outside. Everything's spinning. Dancin' and dancin'; her hands on fire. Damn it, Andres!

ANDRES: What? What's wrong?

WOYZECK: I gotta go. I gotta see.

ANDRES: Is she *worth* all this?

WOYZECK collapses in ANDRES's arms; ANDRES holds him for a beat and then makes him get control of himself.

WOYZECK: I gotta go; it's too hot in here… Let's go.

ANDRES: All right.

SCENE ELEVEN
THE PUB

The DOCTOR enters cross-dressed as a woman, lip-synching. WOYZECK eats his peas against the wall. ANDRES hangs out near the jukebox.

DOCTOR: Ah, Woyzeck, keep eating those peas.

The DRUM MAJOR and SERGEANT enter; they halt as the DOCTOR crosses their path. The DOCTOR bumps into them; the DRUM MAJOR walks away. The DOCTOR dances along behind them until:

SERGEANT: Doc, I do love ya, but…lemme, beat this woman shit outta ya, huh? Come on, Doc. Lemme beat the shit outta this fag thing. I'm a man, ya know. I mean… I wanna break every bone in your body till y' bleed dead.

DOCTOR: Oh my poor little Blue Bird: how is it that the world is so beautiful? I could fill a whole barrel with tears of grief. I wish our noses were bottles so we could empty them down each other's throats.

The DRUM MAJOR and SERGEANT throw knives at the dartboard until MARIE and the others enter. The DRUM MAJOR plays a song on the jukebox and all dance. Within the dance, partners get swapped and the DRUM MAJOR forces MARIE to dance with him.

WOYZECK: Him. Her. DEVIL.

He lunges foward but is stopped by the SERGEANT.

MARIE: (*With the DRUM MAJOR.*) Go go go go go go go go go go go go!

WOYZECK: Go go go go go go go go go go go go! That's right, spin all over the place. Writhe all over each other. Why don't you just blow out the sun, God, and let everything fuck all over the place – man, woman, humans, animals. Do it in broad daylight, do it on the backs of hands like flies. Oh, she's hot. Hot, hot in heat! Go go go go go go go go go go go go!

DRUM MAJOR embraces MARIE right in front of WOYZECK.

Look at him: clawing at her flesh, preying on her body, having her like me. Like I did… Then. In the beginning.

He crumbles to floor and begins to have spasms.

SHOWMAN: (*In WOYZECK's ear.*) All righty then, think you now upon the wanderer who stands poised against the stream of time and all of God's wisdom and dares to ask: 'Wherefore is man? Wherefore is man?' Verily, I say unto thee, how would the farmer, the cooper, the cobbler, the doctor survive if God had not created man? How would the tailor live if God had not implanted in man a sense of shame? And how would the soldier live if God had not equipped man with the need to destroy – to kill? Therefore, do not be afraid. Yes, yes, life is delightful and good. But everything earthly is evil. Everything rots. So piss on the cross and crucify a Jew.

WOYZECK storms out of the pub.

SCENE TWELVE
THE WOODS

WOYZECK: Go go go go go! Go go go go go! (*Singing.*) &$^#%! and *%&#^@! goes the music. Go go go go! Go go go go go! (*He stops.*) Silence! Who's down there? (*He stretches towards the ground.*) Ha? What? What did you say? Louder! Louder! Stab. Stab? Stab the she-wolf. Stab the…she-wolf? Stab the she-wolf dead? Stab the she-wolf dead. Should I? Must I? (*Standing up as though someone lifted him.*) What? Is it there, too? On the wind, as well? Everywhere?

Walking backwards as though someone is pushing him until he arrives at MARIE's window. He turns around to see where he has been led.

Stab her dead. Dead.

WOYZECK climbs through the window and walks to MARIE's door. His hand runs down it; he pulls his hand away and stops himself. He goes to leave; he sees the earrings. He studies them in the moonlight; he places one next to his ear. He pockets the earrings and rushes back to the barracks.

SCENE THIRTEEN
THE BARRACKS

WOYZECK: (*Quietly.*) Andres. Hey, Andres. Andres!

ANDRES: What? What is it, Woyzeck?

WOYZECK: I can't sleep. I… I keep hearing voices, and when I close my eyes, lightning flashes, music screeches and everything spins – go go go go go! And then I see this huge knife hanging in the air, in some sort of dark alley. And there's this crippled man standing behind it. And that's when the voices in the wall start talking to me. Do you hear 'em, Andres?

ANDRES: Take a few tablets with a couple a shots, Woyzeck. That'll stop it.

WOYZECK: They won't stop, Andres, they're everywhere: Stab! Stab! Stab! Stab!

ANDRES: Let it go, Woyzeck. They were just dancing.

WOYZECK alters when he hears this viewpoint.

I'm tired, man; go to sleep… God bless you.

WOYZECK stares at ANDRES, then the earrings in his hand. He looks up.

WOYZECK: Go go go go go go go go go go.

WOYZECK runs to the pub.

SCENE FOURTEEN
THE PUB

DRUM MAJOR: I'm a man. A man, I say! Anybody wanna fight? Huh? That's right, unless you're God Almighty Himself, I suggest you stay the fuck away from me. I'll ram your teeth down to yer shit-hole! I'll /

WOYZECK whistles at the DRUM MAJOR.

Hey boy, drink up! Everybody's got t' drink. I…I wish the world was made of whisky. Whisky.

WOYZECK clips the earrings on DRUM MAJOR and whistles at him.

You little cunt, you want me to rip that tongue outta that faggoty little face and strangle that pussy-girl body with it?

WOYZECK offers the DRUM MAJOR his bottom and whistles again.

When I'm through with you, you worthless piece of shit, you won't have enough wind in you for an old granny's fart.

The DRUM MAJOR beats WOYZECK senseless.

Whistle till ya go blue in the face now, y' useless twat.

WOYZECK: (*After the DRUM MAJOR exits, applauding.*) Yeah, violence.

SCENE FIFTEEN
THE SHOWER ROOM IN THE BARRACKS

WOYZECK crawls across the floor, undresses and pulls out a washing tub. ANDRES enters to bathe.

WOYZECK: Did you hear anything?

ANDRES: He's still in there with the Sarge.

WOYZECK: What did he say?

ANDRES: How do you know he said any /

WOYZECK cuts him off and just looks at him.

Why do you want me to say this?

WOYZECK eyes him again.

All right, he laughed and said… 'She's a real woman – beautiful thighs, and everything so…hot and…wet.'

WOYZECK freezes.

WOYZECK: So that's what he said?

ANDRES: Yeah.

WOYZECK breaks with a haunting sound, collapses into the tub and weeps. ANDRES hesitates and then kneels down to hold and rock WOYZECK like a child. The moment lingers. An unusually loud alarm bell rings.

ANDRES: Come on, Franz, we gotta go to roll-call.

WOYZECK begins to dress but then stops and stares at the bell. WOYZECK becomes dead still and focused. WOYZECK rips the bell off the wall.

Franz! What are you doing?

Silence.

WOYZECK: There was one of her, Andres.

ANDRES: What?

WOYZECK: Nothing. (*He begins to dress in his street clothes.*)
Here, I don't need this anymore. You can have it.

*WOYZECK tosses ANDRES his military coat. WOYZECK then
throws a small box down from the top of a shelf and kicks it to
ANDRES.*

There's a cross in there, it was my little sister's, and
the ring too. There's also a picture of Jesus with a gold
heart. It marked a bit written in my mother's Bible:

> 'Death be my sole reward,
> Despair be my praise to God.
> Lord, as Thy side was red and sore,
> So let my heart be ever more.'

The only thing my mother can feel now is the sun
shining on her hands. She won't miss it.

ANDRES: Franz, we gotta go to roll-call.

WOYZECK: Friedrich Johann Franz Woyzeck, Fusilier, C
Company, 2nd Battalion, 2nd Fusiliers Regiment, born
on the Feast of the Annunciation, the twenty-fifth of
March. I'm thirty years, seven months and twelve days
old today.

ANDRES: You're in a shit state, Franz, go to the doctor – go
sick.

WOYZECK: You know the funny thing is, Andres, when the
carpenter builds the coffin, no one knows who's gonna
lie in it. See ya.

WOYZECK runs away as fast as possible.

SCENE SIXTEEN
THE TRAVELLING SHOWMAN'S, MARIE ON HER OWN
& ROLL-CALL

Three separate scenes played in one space: WOYZECK buys a murder weapon from the TRAVELLING SHOWMAN; roll-call without WOYZECK; and MARIE prays for forgiveness.

SHOWMAN: Well then, Sir, what'll it be?

MARIE: La corruption du siècle est parvenue à un tel point que pour maintenir la morale…

SERGEANT: Stand at. Ease.

Stomp!

WOYZECK: No.

MARIE: (*Opens to* I Peter 2:20.) 'For even hereunto were ye called…'

SERGEANT: Answer your names.

WOYZECK: No.

MARIE: 'Because Christ also suffered for us, leaving us an example, that ye should follow in his footsteps…'

SERGEANT: Fusilier Müller.

MARIE: 'Who did no sin, neither was guile found in his mouth.'

ANDRES: (*Stomp.*) Sergeant.

Stomp.

WOYZECK: No!

SERGEANT: Woyzeck.

WOYZECK: No.

MARIE: 'Who, when he was reviled, reviled not again…'

WOYZECK: No.

MARIE: 'Who, when he suffered, threatened not…'

SERGEANT: WOYZECK!

MARIE: 'But committed himself to him that judgment righteously.'

WOYZECK: OH NO.

MARIE: (*Prays.*) Lord God, Mon Seigneur.

SERGEANT: Where's Woyzeck?

ANDRES: I think he went sick, Sergeant.

WOYZECK: No.

MARIE: Please don't look at me.

SERGEANT: You think he went sick?

ANDRES: Yes Sergeant.

SERGEANT: He's not sick. He's a spineless fucking woman.

MARIE: (*Turns to another page,* John 8:3 *and* 8:11.) 'And the scribes and Pharisees brought unto him a woman taken in adultery and set her in the midst.'

SERGEANT: What's the problem?

MARIE: And Jesus said unto her /

SERGEANT: Answer me, or this drill cane's going down your throat.

MARIE: 'Neither do I condemn thee, go, and sin no more.' (*She clasps her hands together in the prayer position.*)

WOYZECK: No again.

ANDRES: Perhaps he didn't actually go sick, Sergeant.

SERGEANT: Then where is he?

MARIE: Dear God…

ANDRES: I don't know, Sergeant!

MARIE: Mon Dieu! (*Breaking prayer.*)

SERGEANT: Who in the Hell is gonna shave the Captain?

MARIE: (*Crying.*) I can't.

SERGEANT: I said, who the Hell is going t' shave the Captain!?!

The DRUM MAJOR enters. WOYZECK approaches the shaving razor.

WOYZECK: That.

MARIE: Please God.

SERGEANT: Good morning, Sir.

MARIE: Please let me pray.

SERGEANT: With the exception of Fusilier Woyzeck, the C Company is present and awaiting your inspection, Sir.

The BABY screams.

MARIE: Shut up!

WOYZECK: How much for that?

DRUM MAJOR: Where's Woyzeck?

SHOWMAN: It'll cost y' three.

SERGEANT: He went sick, Sir.

WOYZECK: 'S too much.

DRUM MAJOR: Sick chit?

MARIE: You're killing me.

SERGEANT: We don't actually have a sick chit, Sir.

SHOWMAN: You buy or you don't buy.

DRUM MAJOR: What?

SHOWMAN: What'll it be?

SERGEANT: Müller doesn't actually know if he went sick,
Sir.

*WOYZECK turns to see the DRUM MAJOR's knife; the DRUM
MAJOR goes for the bell and discovers the discarded wires on the
ground.*

WOYZECK: How much for the knife?

DRUM MAJOR: Who broke the bell?

MARIE: Where are you Franz?

SHOWMAN: You wanna cut your throat?

SERGEANT: I didn't know it was broken, Sir.

DRUM MAJOR: Who the fuck broke the bell?

SHOWMAN: Hm???

DRUM MAJOR: How I am going to run this place without a
fucking bell?

SHOWMAN: Smart.

DRUM MAJOR: You're going to be my bell, boy. Ring, boy,
RING!!!

SERGEANT: (*Screams like a bell in his highest, most humiliating
falsetto.*)

SHOWMAN: Nice?

SERGEANT: (*Rings.*)

DRUM MAJOR: Yes!

SERGEANT: (*Ringing sound again.*)

DRUM MAJOR: Müller!

ANDRES / SERGEANT: (*Both doing ringing sound.*)

DRUM MAJOR: Louder!

ANDRES / SERGEANT: (*They ring.*)

DRUM MAJOR: Yes!

ANDRES / SERGEANT: (*They ring.*)

DRUM MAJOR: NOW!!!

ANDRES / SERGEANT: (*They ring.*)

DRUM MAJOR: Who the fuck is gonna shave the Captain?

SHOWMAN: I'll give it to you cheaper than anywhere else.

DRUM MAJOR: SOMEBODY HAS TO SHAVE THE FUCKIN' CAPTAIN.

MARIE: COME HOME FRANZ.

Stillness and silence.

DRUM MAJOR: You?

SHOWMAN: You can have your death cheap, huh?

MARIE: Come home.

DRUM MAJOR: I don't think so.

SHOWMAN: But not for free.

DRUM MAJOR: Get out of my fucking sight.

MARIE: Please.

DRUM MAJOR: And don't show your faces around me again until Woyzeck's face is next to it and the Captain's face is as smooth as your faggoty shaved chest.

SHOWMAN: (*Beat.*) What'll it be?

SERGEANT / ANDRES: Yes Sir.

DRUM MAJOR: I'll inform the Captain.

MARIE: It's hot, too hot.

DRUM MAJOR: DISS! MISSED.

The DRUM MAJOR, SERGEANT and ANDRES exit.

MARIE: I'm suffocating.

SHOWMAN: You can have your death at a discount.

WOYZECK: Go go go go go go go.

SHOWMAN: It'll cost you two.

MARIE: Everything's dead inside.

SHOWMAN: What'll it be?

WOYZECK: There.

WOYZECK gives the SHOWMAN two coins.

SHOWMAN: There. Like money was nothing. Dog.

The SHOWMAN clears away the remaining murder weapons and exits.

MARIE: Help.

SCENE SEVENTEEN
THE WASHING ROOM

The ladies wash.

MARGARET: (*Singing a Welsh spiritual.*)
      Nidwyn gofyn, bowyd moethys.
      Aer y byd nai berlair mân.
      Gofyn rwyf am calon hapus, calon onest, calon lân.
      Calon lân yn llawn diony.
      Tecachyw nar lilyr dlos.
      Does on calon lân all ganu.
      Canu'r dydd a canu'r nos.

GRANDMOTHER: You can't sing.

MARGARET: Well, you're the one who asked me to.

GRANDMOTHER: You sing, Marie.

MARIE: I can't.

MARGARET: Why not?

MARIE: Because.

MARGARET: Because what?

MARIE: Tell us a story, Grandma.

GRANDMOTHER: Me? Really? All right. Sit down. Sit.
Once upon a time, there was a poor child who had
no father and no mother, everyone was dead, and
there was nothing left in the world. And even though
everything was dead, the child searched for life day and
night. But when the child found that nobody *was* left on
the earth, the child wanted to go to Heaven because the
moon smiled down at him so friendly. And when at last
he arrived at the moon, he discovered it was just a piece
of rotten wood. And so he went to the sun, but when he

got to the sun, it was just a wilted sunflower. And when he got to the stars, they were just dead fireflies, smeared on the sky. And so he wanted to go back to the earth again, but discovered it was just an empty, overturned pot. And so he was all alone. And he sat down and cried. And he's still sitting there. Alone.

WOYZECK: (*Standing in a doorway with a picnic hamper.*) Maria.

MARIE: (*Startled.*) What?

WOYZECK: It's time t' go.

MARIE: What time is it?

WOYZECK: I don't know.

MARIE: Where are we going?

WOYZECK: I don't know.

MARIE gives the BABY to GRANDMOTHER, kisses her and has a moment with MARGARET. She exits with WOYZECK. GRANDMOTHER and MARGARET rush off.

SCENE EIGHTEEN
THE WOODS

MARIE: Town's that way… It's going t' get dark soon…

WOYZECK: We're staying a while. Come here.

MARIE: I should go.

WOYZECK: I'm not gonna let your feet get sore from walking.

MARIE: Franz…

WOYZECK: Do you know how long it's been, Marie?

MARIE: (*Beat.*) It'll be two years this Easter.

WOYZECK: And do you know how much longer it'll be?

MARIE: I need to get back to Christian, Franz.

WOYZECK: Are you cold, Marie? And yet you're warm, aren't you. Those hot lips. That hot, hot whore's-breath. And yet I'd give the whole of the Heavens to kiss them again. Are you cold? When you're cold, you won't *feel* cold anymore. You won't feel cold in the morning dew.

MARIE: Franz, what do you want to say?

WOYZECK: Nothing. (*He falls silent.*)

MARIE: Moon's coming up: red as red…

WOYZECK: 'And the sun became black…and the moon became as blood.' (*From* Revelations 6:12.)

MARIE: What's going on, Franz? You're pale.

He turns and almost kisses her. Then he shoves her against the wall and begins to stab her.

WOYZECK: Die, die, die, die, die, die, die, die, DIE!!!

He stabs her heart.

Take that and that and that and that! DIIIIIIEEEEEEE.

Her body falls to the ground, reaching for him, pleading with him to stop.

Still moving? Still not dead? Not yet?

He stabs all over her back like a crazed butcher – about thirty times – with increasing speed until he's like a jackhammer. He yanks her over.

Are you dead yet? Are you dead?

The white blanket she's on begins to glow blood-red.

Dead. Dead.

Music. Couples begin to slow dance and re-form the pub. WOYZECK returns to the pub.

SCENE NINETEEN
THE PUB

WOYZECK hits the jukebox; another song plays. He hits it again; another song; he hits it a third time; another song. He rips the cord out from it and tosses it onto the floor.

ANDRES: Woyzeck.

SERGEANT: Woyzeck.

DRUM MAJOR: Woyzeck.

The SERGEANT and DRUM MAJOR step towards WOYZECK. WOYZECK runs and bounds off the wall all over the space.

WOYZECK: Come on everybody, let's dance! Go go go go go! Go! GO! GO! Go! (*Hanging from the knife-board on the wall.*) Come on, come on: sweat all over the place; fill the room with y' nasty stench: sweat and stink, sweat and stink! (*Standing in the window.*) The Devil's coming for us all in the end anyway!

He grabs MARGARET and pulls her onto the dance floor.

Come on, Margaret! This is no time for sittin' down! I'm hot!!! HOT!!! It's like this, Mags, the Devil takes one and lets another one go. Oh! – Peggy – you're hot! (*Whispering into her ear from behind as they both stare at the DRUM MAJOR.*) And why's that I wonder? Yes, Maggie, you, too, will be cold some day. Careful!!! Come on, dance with me now!

MARGARET struggles free of WOYZECK. The DRUM MAJOR and SERGEANT go towards him; WOYZECK takes his BABY from GRANDMOTHER; all step back. WOYZECK's movement becomes very light and beautiful, almost like flying – he rocks the BABY about the space over the following.

MARGARET: What's that on your hands?

WOYZECK: (*Still dancing with BABY.*) Me?

MARGARET: It's blood. That's blood.

WOYZECK: Blood?

MARGARET: Blood!

WOYZECK: (*Laughing and waving it at others.*) I must have cut my hand.

MARGARET: Then how come it's on your elbow?

WOYZECK: I must have wiped it off.

MARGARET: You wiped your right hand on your right elbow? That's talent.

GRANDMOTHER: 'And then the Giant said: "Fee fie fo fum, I smell the blood of a dead wo-mun. And it stinks."'

WOYZECK: Devil! What do you want? What are you doing? Gimme some space, or I'll / Devil! What d' y' think, I killed someone? You think I'm some kind of murderer? What're you staring at!?! *LOOK AT YOUR SELVES. LOOK AT YOUR OWN SELVES!!!* Gimme some space!

WOYZECK runs out. All follow.

SCENE TWENTY
THE WOODS

A storm of noise; WOYZECK runs as fast as humanly possible.

WOYZECK: The knife. Where's the knife? I left it there;
it'll betray me. Warmer and warmer. Ugh, where
am I? Misty grey all around. (*Noise.*) What's that?
Beetles cracking like broken bells. (*Silence and stillness.*)
Something's moving. Quiet! – just there. There. Marie?
Ah! – Marie! Silent. Everything's so silent: cold, wet and
still. Look at your hair, Marie; it's gone all wild. Haven't
you brushed it today? And what's that around your
neck? That red necklace. What sins did you commit
t' earn that, Marie, huh? Oh, you were black with sin.
BLACK ALL OVER. Did I make you white again? Did
I make you white?

I've gotta get outta here. The knife, the knife! Where
is it…? Here: yes! Now…where where where where
where?

WOYZECK exits the space. The lights focus on MARIE's corpse.
WOYZECK reappears at the edge of a pond.

Sink down, deep down: (*He releases the knife.*) Blue water,
bloody moon. It won't be deep enough; they'll find it
this summer when they're swimming. (*He gropes for the*
knife.) And what about when they're diving? (*He gropes*
again.) No. It'll rust and they won't be able to recognize
it. Damn it! I should've broken it into a thousand little
pieces! (*He gropes again – height of paranoia.*) Ah! I can't
find it. Everything's working against me. I'm wet; I'm
cold; I'm bloody. I'm / Oh, I'm coated in blood. Wet
blood all over. I've have t' / I have t' wash myself. I
have to clean. There's a stain and there's a stain and
– Stain. Stain. Stain. Stain. What'll they say? What'll

they all say? What'll they say, what'll they do, what'll they... Do. Do. What'll they do?

MARIE's blanket glows with blood again.

I'm sorry, I'm sorry, I... I...

The full ensemble enter into WOYZECK's mind. ANDRES shaves the CAPTAIN who laughs and laughs. The DRUM MAJOR has sex with MARGARET. The SERGEANT dances with the jukebox. GRANDMOTHER alone. The DOCTOR dissects MARIE's corpse. The SHOWMAN leaving town... Chaos. It rains peas. Then, in one beat, all stops.

I.

WOYZECK drowns himself. Snap to black.

The End.